READING POWER

High-Tech Vehicles

Bullet Trains

William Amato

The Rosen Publishing Group's
PowerKids Press™
New York

JL CDS

Published in 2002 by The Rosen Publishing Group, Inc.
29 East 21st Street, New York, NY 10010

First Edition

Book Design: Christopher Logan

Photo Credits: Cover, pp. 18–19 © Robert Holmes/Corbis; pp. 4–5 © Dallas and John Heaton/Corbis; pp. 6–7 © Craig Lovell/Corbis; pp. 8–9 © Chris Rainier/Corbis; pp. 10–11 © FPG International; pp. 12–13 © Dean Conger/Corbis; p. 13 (inset) © Markus Schreiber/AP/Wide World Photos; pp. 14–15, 17 (top) © Milepost 92½/Corbis; p. 17 (bottom) © David Zalubowski/AP/Wide World Photos; pp. 20–21 © Reuters NewMedia, Inc./Corbis

Amato, William.
Bullet trains / William Amato.
    p. cm. — (High-tech vehicles)
ISBN 0-8239-6008-0
1. High speed trains–Juvenile literature. [1. High speed trains. 2. Railroads–Trains.] I. Title.
TF1450 .A43 2001
385'.2—dc21

                                            2001000272

Manufactured in the United States of America

Contents

Bullet Trains

Bullet trains are high-tech vehicles. Most bullet trains travel more than 150 miles an hour. They carry people a long way in a very short time.

Japan was the first country to use bullet trains.

Bullet Train Speeds

Country	Train Name	Top Speed
France	*TGV*	186 miles an hour
Japan	*Shinkansen*	186 miles an hour
Germany	*ICE*	173 miles an hour
United States	*Acela Express*	150 miles an hour

Bullet trains have big electric engines. The engine is in the front car of the train.

Engine

A bullet train has a long nose. It looks like the nose of a jet plane. A long nose helps the train go faster. Bullet trains also are called high-speed trains.

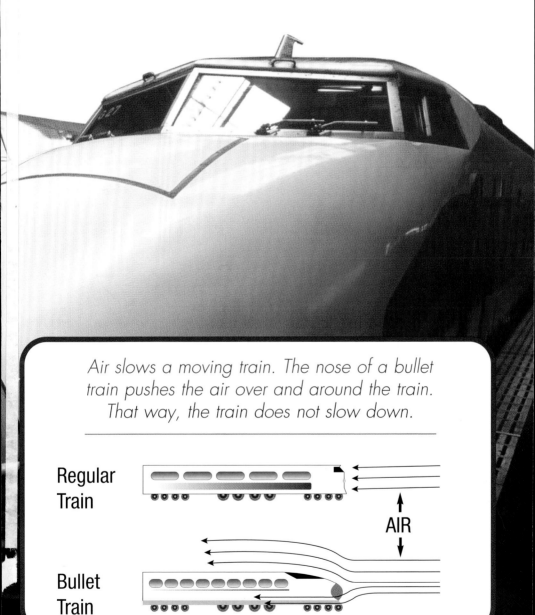

Air slows a moving train. The nose of a bullet train pushes the air over and around the train. That way, the train does not slow down.

Regular Train

Bullet Train

AIR

Bullet trains are made of light metal. Light trains go faster than heavy trains. Bullet trains go so fast that everything around them looks blurry.

IT'S A FACT!

Some bullet train engine cars weigh ten tons less than locomotives of the past.

Riding the Rails

The tracks of a bullet train are built on flat land. They must be as straight as possible.

The tracks that a bullet train runs on are smooth. Smooth tracks help bullet trains go faster.

Trains tilt when they go around a curve. Bullet trains are made so that people don't feel it when the train tilts.

Driving Bullet Trains

Computers help engineers drive bullet trains. Computers help control the train's speed.

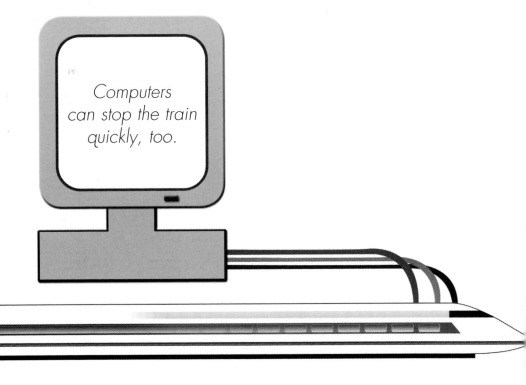

Computers can stop the train quickly, too.

This man (left) is learning how to drive a bullet train.

Traveling in Style

Riding in a bullet train is very comfortable. The cars are made so that they do not shake at high speeds. They are made to keep out the noise of the train as it moves.

Speeding into the Future

This new Japanese train can go 300 miles an hour. Soon, some trains will go even faster.

Glossary

engine (**ehn**-juhn) a machine that is used to power vehicles

locomotives (loh-kuh-**moh**-tihvz) large engines that move under their own power and are used to pull railroad trains

tilt (**tihlt**) the leaning movement of a train as it goes around a curve

tracks (**traks**) metal rails that the wheels of a train run on

Resources

Books

Trains
by Jon Richards
Millbrook Press (1998)

Trains
by Joy Richardson
Franklin Watts, Inc. (1994)

Web Site

National Geographic
http://www.nationalgeographic.com/
    traveler/archive/2000-07-3-0.html

Index

Word Count: 216

Note to Librarians, Teachers, and Parents

If reading is a challenge, Reading Power is a solution! Reading Power is perfect for readers who want high-interest subject matter at an accessible reading level. These fact-filled, photo-illustrated books are designed for readers who want straightforward vocabulary, engaging topics, and a manageable reading experience. With clear picture/text correspondence, leveled Reading Power books put the reader in charge. Now readers have the power to get the information they want and the skills they need in a user-friendly format.